Vintage
Shops
LONDON

Vintage Shops

LONDON

Featuring more than 50 vintage shops,
markets and stalls

Michelle Mason

PIMPERNEL
PRESS LTD
www.pimpernelpress.com

About the author

Michelle Mason is a designer,
shopkeeper and stylist and has
worked for a number of clients
including Sir John Soane's Museum
shop, the British Library, the
National Gallery and the Southbank
Centre. She is also co-founder of
east London vintage shop Mason &
Painter in Columbia Road, home to
the weekly Sunday Flower Market.

Vintage Shops London is her second
book and was inspired by a desire
to champion independent vintage
stores and antiques markets and to
offer readers a glimpse into what's
on offer in the UK's capital.

Pimpernel Press Limited
www.pimpernelpress.com

Vintage Shops London
© Pimpernel Press Limited 2021
Text and photographs © Michelle Mason 2021 except
for those listed on page 144

A catalogue record for this book is available
from the British Library.

ISBN 978-1-910258-99-6

Typeset in Excelsior MT
Printed and bound in China
by C&C Offset Printing Company Limited

9 8 7 6 5 4 3 2 1

Contents

Introduction

As an antidote to throwaway culture, non-sustainable products and fast fashion, in *Vintage Shops London* I take a look at some of my favourite bricks and mortar vintage shops and uncover some new ones along the way. These small independent businesses represent the real and fun experience of shopping and if, like me, you love the discovery of a new boutique, the physical experience of the location, the displays and the adventure of sourcing reclaimed and repurposed objects, chances are you enjoy browsing vintage shops and flea markets and encountering the new within the old.

Whether you are kitting out your home or your wardrobe, or simply looking for an unusual gift, this book takes a look at some of the most inspiring vintage and antiques shops and markets within London.

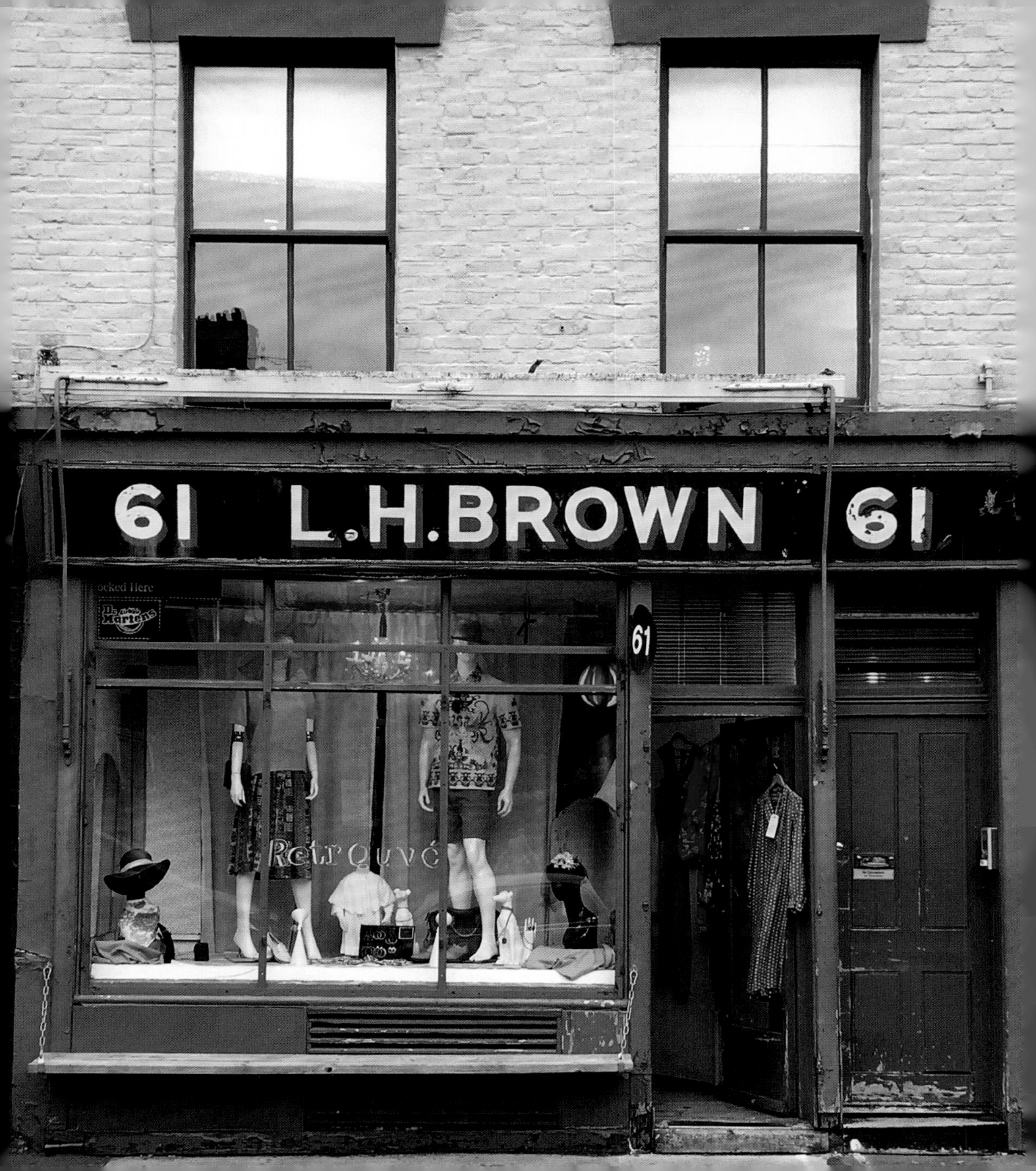
61 L.H.BROWN 61
61
Retrouvé

Londoners love nothing more than the unexpected discovery of a one-off find. The desire to smoke out a great pre-loved bargain is undoubtedly fuelled by the abundance of quirky, good quality outlets across the capital.

Whether browsing salvage yards, such as Lassco in Vauxhall, for reclaimed doors or delving into a maze of forgotten treasure in Portobello Road the hunt for the real McCoy has become a favourite weekend pastime for many city folk.

Throughout the book I've highlighted some of London's favourite vintage emporiums and markets. Each shop is profiled with a description of what it is best known for with photographs of inspiring displays to tempt you throughout, plus there is a chapter on how to recreate your own 'vintage look'. I hope you enjoy exploring these independent shops as much as I've enjoyed featuring them.

LONDON STYLE

Vintage Shops London is arranged in sections: north, south, east, west and central which includes the City; from the unique industrial style of London's east end, the painted shop fronts on Portobello Market in the west, the thrift shops of north London and salvage yards south of the river and the history of the City of London. It is well worth exploring the many styles and characters that London has to offer.

A slow brunch in Borough Market, a stroll along the river and a snoop round Vinegar Yard, spying vintage shops and cosy cafés, is my idea of the best way to spend time in London: away from the crowds and rush hour traffic. These images capture the moments and the atmosphere beyond the tourist hotspots and monuments where you can discover the small, individual boutiques, vintage stores and charity shops.

NORTH LONDON

Camden Passage Antiques Market

ISLINGTON

Camden Passage Antiques Market, Islington, N1 8AE
www.camdenpassageislington.co.uk
The market runs every Wednesday from 10am.
Check individual shop opening times before heading out.

Camden Passage, Islington, is a quaint pedestrian-only street known for its pretty cafés, bars and vintage boutiques and every Wednesday a bustling outdoor antiques market adds to the charm. It's worth going early as the stalls set up to catch the best finds from flea market bargains to vintage clothes, old letterpress type, antique jewellery, lace and textiles and coins. There are several bric-a-brac stalls where prices are very reasonable.

The specialist antiques shops running along the street and into adjacent **Pierrepont Arcade** are filled with high-end collectors' items that include art nouveau glassware, art deco jewellery, crystal champagne glasses and decanters, silver tea sets, arts and crafts ceramics, furniture and costume jewellery. A favourite of mine is **Number One** on Pierrepont Arcade, where you'll find crockery from every era including Georgian tea sets, original Willow pattern plates, full Victorian dinner services and assorted bargains on the heaving tables outside.

Back on Camden Passage, at number 12, you'll find **Annie's** where owner Annie has sold vintage clothing since the 1970s after being inspired by the character Annie Hall and her quirky dress sense in the eponymous Woody Allen film.

Adored by London's fashion designers and celebrities Annie's boutique specializes in off-beat vintage dresses, feather capes, Victorian petticoats, embroidered shawls and a large selection of original lace wedding dresses from the 1920s.

The shops in Camden Passage cover a range of specialist antiques and vintage items from silverware, tea sets (right), Lalique glass, coins and vintage costume jewellery to original typesetter's blocks (above).

Flashback Records

ESSEX ROAD

Flashback Records, Islington – 50 Essex Road, N1 8LR
also at:
Crouch End – 144 Crouch Hill, N8 9DX
Shoreditch – 131 Bethnal Green Road, E2 7DG
www.flashback.co.uk

On Essex Road you'll find Flashback Records where owner Mark Burgess set up this original store in 1997 to sell vintage vinyl and CDs. Now firmly on the map with a following of loyal customers, the Islington shop offers sections dedicated to all genres including 1950s and 1960s rock & pop, jazz, reggae, hip hop and soul in the basement whilst the ground floor is a treasure trove of second-hand CDs and videos. On a fine day wooden crates are wheeled on to the pavement to tempt you with their extensive selection of second-hand singles and LPs and lead you inside where you'll discover, in their own words, 'a crate digger's paradise'.

Since its inception, in the late 1990s, two more branches of Flashback have opened their doors to customers eager to fill gaps in their record collections; a little further north, in **Crouch End** and east in **Shoreditch** where the two storey store is packed to the rafters with a collection to rival the original Islington branch. The Shoreditch branch also hosts gigs by both well-known and up-and-coming artists.

Past Caring

ESSEX ROAD

54 Essex Road, Islington, N1 8LR

Filled with the kind of flea market finds that attract food stylists and prop buyers this Islington second-hand shop has been one of north London's best kept vintage secrets since the 1970s. Expect to find little hidden treasures such as 1960s Whitefriars glassware and mid-century Stoke-on-Trent collectables from ceramic artists Jessie Tate and Susie Cooper.

Furniture, vintage paintings, pre-loved record players, and rocking horses are stacked outside on the pavement together with dining chairs, mannequins and items of vintage clothing. The shop's basement is also worth delving into for furniture and has a good selection of second-hand desks, tables, armchairs, artworks and larger paintings.

The owner Carl and his staff are very approachable and on hand to answer any questions. Be warned, this shop doesn't do minimal.

An eclectic mix of 1970s glassware and a vintage framed print of London Beefeaters.

Camden Market

CAMDEN TOWN

Camden Market, Camden Lock Place,
Camden Town, NW1 8AF
www.camdenmarket.com
Everyday 10am–late, times may vary for each business

Any mention of London's vintage markets would have to include Camden and the area around Regent's Canal known as Camden Lock where a vintage and crafts market has drawn huge crowds since the 1970s. Much of the original vintage market and stables have been taken over in recent times by food and drink stalls but Camden is still very much a go-to destination for vintage and second-hand clothes. With successful independent vintage clothing shops such as **Rokit** and **Vintage Planet** plus a multitude of stalls, there are still plenty of vintage rails to rummage through and lots of individual pitches.

Rokit

CAMDEN TOWN

225 Camden High St, Camden Town, NW1 7BU
also at:
Rokit, 101 Brick Lane, E1 6SE
Rokit Originals Boutique, 107 Brick Lane, E1 6SE
Rokit Covent Garden, 42 Shelton Street, WC2H 9HZ
www.rokit.co.uk

Rokit started out as a Camden market stall over thirty years ago selling vintage American denim. Since then they have established four brick-and-mortar shops, with the original outpost still on Camden High Street where you'll find a full spectrum of vintage and sustainable fashion. Their men and women's Gold Collection includes rare vintage and designer collectables such as 1940s dresses, 1950s leather bikers' jackets, unique designer garments, branded pre-loved sportswear and tee-shirts, vintage Levis, ex-military garments as well as accessories and fashion-inspired books.

You may also like
VINTAGE PLANET
D23 Camden Stables, Camden High Street, NW1 8QP
www.vintageplanetlondon.com

The Black Gull Bookshop & Bindery

CAMDEN TOWN

70–71 West Yard, Camden Lock Place,
Camden Town, NW1 8AF
www.camdenmarket.com

Another favourite at Camden Lock is The Black Gull Bookshop & Bindery where you could easily lose an hour browsing the shelves for second-hand gems and collectable vintage books. There are boxes outside on the cobbles at bargain prices and a good children's section as well as the usual second-hand paperbacks, novels and cookbooks. And if you have a book spine that needs a quick fix then drop it in at their in-house bindery where they will happily sort it out for you.

CHATSWORTH ROAD

7 Chatsworth Road,
E5 0LH

At the gritty end of Chatsworth Road, in the north east of the city, amongst fast food takeaways and laptop repair shops you'll find Patina, a tiny shop, run by friendly husband and wife team Robert and Ula. This gem of a store sells French 'brocante' tableware, paintings, prints and a large selection of pretty vintage glassware, as well as antique Ukrainian pottery decorated with rustic motifs, and combines an assorted mix of vintage bakeware, Polish linen dresses and ceramics and Japanese Kokeshi dolls. No surface or floor space is left empty and stock is lovingly stacked under the canopy outside; old metal bathtubs used for garden planters, reclaimed stripy deckchairs and vintage terracotta plant pots are plentiful.

If you're looking for an unusual second-hand gift, a treat for yourself or thinking of furnishing your kitchen cupboards with beautiful vintage tableware then Patina is a must.

The shop's owner Robert, above, can often be found outside the shop arranging stock and informing customers of new finds. Crates of plant pots surround the doorway together with reclaimed Polish dresses, an artist's easel and a collection of Japanese Kokeshi dolls in the window. A peek through the door, left, shows a view of the interior and an assorted mix of toys, vintage lighting, picture frames, 1970s ceramics and a cupboard full of sparkling antique French wine glasses.

PAPER BAC

PRICE
TICKETS
of every description

PRINTED BAGS
&
CARRIERS
TO ORDER

SOUTH LONDON

Lassco Brunswick House

VAUXHALL

30 Wandsworth Road, Vauxhall, SW8 2LG
www.lassco.co.uk

If you're on the hunt for architectural antiques and salvage with history then Lassco is *the* place to visit. Housed in a Georgian mansion opposite what would have been the illustrious Vauxhall Pleasure Gardens this beautifully restored building is now home to an extensive selection of antiques where silk drapes frame pillared doorways, vintage paintings decorate panelled walls and crystal chandeliers illuminate original Georgian features within its spacious rooms.

You'll be spoilt for choice; as well as a vast array of antique furniture you'll come across restored light fittings, mirrors, tiles from French farmhouses, historical fireplaces, statuary, garden salvage, decorative reclamation and salvaged floorboard stock, including parquet floors and timber rescued from historic buildings and demolition sites.

If you don't have the space or budget for sizable antiques do make sure you pay a visit to their restaurant and garden café for inspiration whilst surrounded by Georgian grandeur and eclectic salvage.

Flea at Vinegar Yard

BERMONDSEY

Vinegar Yard, St Thomas St, Bermondsey, SE1 3QU
www.flealondon.com
Open weekends, check ahead for venue access

The ever-changing area around Bermondsey and Borough Food Market is becoming a mecca for new restaurants, cafés and pop-ups and Flea at Vinegar Yard is no exception. This quirky venue consists of old train carriages, brimming with individual traders ranging from food to vintage clothes, records and fleamarket finds. Everything from 1970s leather coats to reclaimed shop signs, vintage ceramics, books and cameras can be picked up for a reasonable price.

Just a short hop from London Bridge station and the Shard the open-air yard is a perfect spot in the warmer months. Plenty of outdoor seating and a choice of food stalls make this a great spot to brunch and browse for pre-loved vintage finds.

Vintique London

PECKHAM

Unit 13 Station Passage, Queen's Road,
SE15 2JR
www.vintiquelondon.co.uk
Open Saturday 10am–5pm, Sunday 11am–5pm

To call Vintique London a second-hand furniture shop would be doing it an injustice. Since 2012, owner Howard has built up a wide and dedicated collection of mid and later twentieth-century furniture and accessories. Arranged warehouse-style in a railway arch below Queen's Road Station, Peckham, this large but well organized stock of industrial, retro and vintage has everything from dining tables, record cabinets, bookshelves and chests of drawers to smaller pieces such as side tables and 1970s floor lamps.

With highly sought-after brands such as G Plan and Ercol, two of the leading British furniture manufacturers in the 1950s, as well as Scandinavian collectables from Benny Linden and Egon Ostergaard there are some real gems to be had. Also look out for stylish 1960s Sutcliffe sideboards, bookcases, Anglepoise lamps and mirrors.

Described in their own words as, 'a treasure trove', Vintique London is a must if you're a fan of good quality, well-priced mid-century design.

EAST LONDON

Paper Dress Vintage

HACKNEY

352a Mare St, E8 1HR
www.paperdressvintage.co.uk

If you're looking for well-priced, quirky vintage clothes then this Hackney Central boutique is definitely worth a visit. Owner Hannah sources a variety of mainly British stock dating from 1900 to the 1980s. You'll find both men's and women's fashion spread over two floors, as well as a wide selection of accessories including jewellery, handbags, belts, ties and hats.

Hannah's sense of fun and style is reflected in the wide range of clothes she selects, from exquisite beaded flapper dresses and 1930s silk slip dresses to 1950s cashmere cardigans and zany 1970s shirts. The website is also well worth browsing as it offers a useful timeline of vintage outfits and fashions.

And that's not all. After sourcing an outfit from your favourite decade you can party the night away, with a cocktail or craft beer in hand, as Paper Dress becomes a bar and event space by night. The upstairs space is host to a vibrant live music scene and independent venue with guest DJs, a fully stocked bar, dance floor complete with 1960s-inspired monochrome tiles, and a courtyard outside to enjoy summer nights al fresco.

Vintage Heaven

SHOREDITCH

82 Columbia Rd, E2 7QB
www.vintageheaven.co.uk

When a vintage shop has a tearoom at the back you just know you've stumbled on to something good – especially when their home-made cakes are served on 1950s rose-patterned plates and the walls are crammed with pre-loved art and quirky 1970s prints.

Welcome to Vintage Heaven where Margaret, owner and buyer, lovingly curates an eclectic mix of quality tableware and serveware ranging from 1940s tea sets, complete mid-century dinner services, 1960s studio glassware and vintage linens and tablecloths. It's the sort of shop that reminds me of my grandmother's kitchen: welcoming, friendly and familiar. Margaret has curated some seriously collectable pieces throughout her forty-plus years of 'harvesting other people's unwanted possessions,' as she fondly puts it.

Visit the Columbia Road shop for a wide choice of decorative items and vintage kitchenware from a single teacup to rare finds including Ercol stick back Windsor chairs and the aforementioned Scandinavian studio glass.

B Southgate Vintage

SHOREDITCH

4 The Courtyard, Ezra St, E2 7RH
www.bsouthgate.co.uk

The late Victorian buildings that surround Ben Southgate's shop were once home to a row of upholstery workrooms servicing the booming furniture trade a few streets away in Shoreditch. Almost a century later, with the industry long gone, it seems fitting that Ben opened his vintage furniture business in one of the restored workshops steeped in local history.

Ben has a reputation for sourcing quality antiques and mid-century furniture ranging from around 1900 to 1950. He trained as an architect then worked as a furniture restorer before setting up his own business sourcing and refurbishing vintage furniture.

Londoners in the know visit his east London shop to buy from the ready-to-enjoy stock that Ben has lovingly restored using his specialist knowledge from re-wiring lamps, to upholstering antique chairs and easing drawers on time-worn cabinets. Stock is predominantly French with some British, Italian, Czech and Dutch pieces and varies to suit all budgets from candlesticks to 1920s daybeds.

Ben's shop is a wonderful collection of fully restored items including armchairs, dining tables, French school chairs, vintage lamps and lighting and old haberdashery cabinets.

Town House

SPITALFIELDS

5 Fournier Street, E1 6QE
www.townhousespitalfields.com

If the walls of this compelling Georgian house could talk they would tell you stories of its past residents: the French Huguenot immigrants, the Irish weavers and silk merchants, as well as of the many cultural shifts that the area around old Spitalfields market has witnessed. Town House was built in the 1720s but by the 1990s the area was run down and the house had deteriorated. Current owner, Fiona Atkins, bought the property in the late nineties, restoring it to its former glory and basing her antiques business on the lower floors.

Today the shop brims with antique furniture, displays of hand-painted ceramics and one-of-a-kind pieces including apothecary bottles from old chemist shops, books and vintage artworks. Fiona specializes in French terracotta pots with colour-splash glazes; the highly collectable greens are her personal favourite and originate from Vaucluse in the southeast of France.

Table tops filled with vintage, hand-decorated pottery from France where Fiona sources much of her stock.

TAKE A BREAK

Below the shop, in the original basement kitchen, you'll find the coffee shop serving home-made cakes, teas and coffee. An arched recess, where the kitchen stove once stood, is decorated with delft tiles and a myriad of vintage copper cooking pans – impressions of a once bustling Georgian home. It's easy to forget that London's busy financial district is just streets away. Let Fournier Street and the Town House instantly transport you to Georgian London.

Upstairs and at the back of the antiques shop is a small paved patio and garden room – originally installed by a doctor in the 1850s to use as his surgery – where Fiona now houses contemporary art exhibitions and sells vintage British art from 1900 to 1960.

The beautifully restored Town House is testament to Fiona's knowledge and experience; as a young child she was taken to auctions and antiques shops by her antiques dealer parents and later she joined the family business.

Outside, facing the Georgian Hawksmoor church, it's easy to see why this historical street is constantly photographed and it may have something to do with the beautifully arranged displays of antiques in Town House's handsome windows and the eye-catching wooden bicycle leaning by the front door.

Retrouvé

BROADWAY MARKET

23 Broadway Market, E8 4PH
also at:
61 Wilton Way, E8 1BS
www.retrouvevintage.co.uk

Discovering a hoard of clothes in her grandmother's attic was the start of a lifelong passion for vintage clothes and sustainable fashion for Ginny Burnett, owner of Retrouvé. Sourcing original vintage pieces is now a full-time job and takes Ginny around the country as well as on regular trips to France. She opened her first shop in 2013, on **Wilton Way** close to leafy London Fields and with a second, larger branch of Retrouvé now open on **Broadway Market** there is more space to display the collections. With everything from vintage Japanese kimonos to glam seventies maxi dresses and 1930s tea dresses Retrouvé has built a reputation for offering a personal one-to-one experience and provides an in-house alteration service.

Ginny works with the seasons and regularly dresses the double-fronted windows in the Broadway Market shop with seasonal stock where you can expect to see vintage swimwear and silk blouses in the summer, interspersed with romantic vintage bridal wear, to jumpsuits, coats and knitwear during the cooler months. With designer pieces including collectable British seventies brands such as Biba and Ossie Clark you can count on some quality finds.

The decoration in both shops is eclectic and bohemian glam with deco-inspired palm tree wallpaper and vintage haberdashery counters with displays of pre-loved hats, gloves and handbags.

Pure White Lines at Mare Street Market

HACKNEY
117 Mare Street, E8 4RU
www.purewhitelines.com
www.marestreetmarket.com

The building that now houses the eponymous Mare Street Market was built in the 1960s and originally used by Hackney Council as office space. With large crittall style windows, raw concrete walls and tall ceilings the interior is transformed – stripped of its interior walls and ceiling space – to create a large, open-plan marketplace.

Rows of vintage chandeliers and lanterns bounce light across the bar and dining area and the in-house vintage emporium, Pure White Lines, has created a walk-through antiques shop filled with reclaimed industrial salvage, mirrors, taxidermy, vintage furniture and carved stone statues. The collections spill across the market's interior, which is also home to an independent florist, traditional barber, record shop and deli.

The sheer size of the building is jaw dropping and the majestic scale of the antiques – salvaged from old banks, shops and museums – create a dramatic, decorative space worthy of a movie set except that every piece is for sale.

Hunky Dory

BRICK LANE

226 Brick Lane, E1 6SA
www.hunkydoryvintage.com

In a prime position at the top of Brick Lane, a street famous for its markets, bagel bakeries and Indian restaurants, you'll find Hunky Dory Vintage, a boutique dedicated to both men's and women's vintage clothing. The dapper shop front always has a stop-and-stare window display and Hunky Dory's owner, Ian, describes the collections as classic vintage. He supplies a wide following of committed customers with original Harris Tweed jackets, vintage Levis, two piece suits and French workwear as well as glamorous ball gowns and American vintage cheerleader jackets.

Ian has a knack for sourcing prime thirties, forties and fifties clothes and the highly sought-after 'bleu de travail' – blue dyed vintage French workwear are in constant supply as well as vintage leather jackets and quirky 1950s prints. If you've found it difficult to locate good quality men's originals, then look no further; Hunky Dory will definitely help to fill all the gaps.

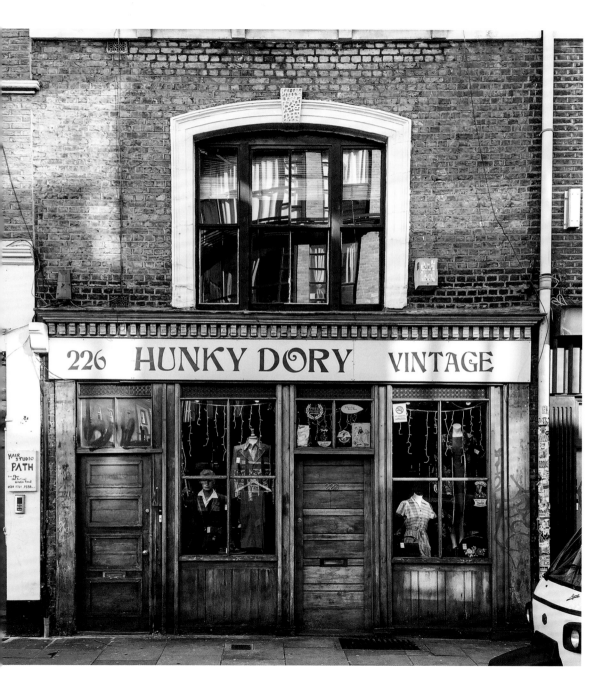

Straw London

SHOREDITCH

126 Columbia Road, E2 7RG
www.strawlondon.co.uk

Wicker baskets, straw hats and charming string shopping bags dangle from wooden peg-racks along with shelves crammed with hand-thrown terracotta mugs, vintage dairy bowls and checked tablecloths. It's a scene that conjures up images of an old farmhouse kitchen from a time when beautiful objects were lovingly crafted for everyday use.

Straw London started out as a personal passion for owner Emily but after her collection of straw bags and vintage baskets began to take over her living space, she decided to set up shop and turned a hobby into a business.

Emily's search for unique hand-crafted pieces regularly takes her to France where she sources much of the stock including (overleaf) vintage brooms and baskets, cane carpet beaters, 1970s string shoppers, hand-thrown ceramics and vintage peasant tops.

Emily's originality and talent for detail is evident in the welcoming displays that she creates in her beautifully curated shop.

An assortment of re-claimed wicker baskets, vintage straw bags, brooms and shopping baskets at Straw London.

WEST LONDON

Alfies Antique Market

MARYLEBONE

13–25 Church St, NW8 8DT
alfiesantiques.com

Step into this former art deco department store in Marylebone and you'll instantly be transported to a world of Bauhaus-inspired interiors, arts and crafts furniture and beaded flapper dresses. The antique art collection at one entrance, dazzling twentieth-century lighting at another and 1920s costumes and accessories through the east door are tasters of the many delights within. Alfies Antique Market covers such a wide range of antiques and collectable vintage that it's almost impossible to see it all in one visit.

If you have just a couple of hours start with **Tin Tin** clothes and accessories on the ground floor, where you'll see beautiful vintage gowns, 1930s lamé evening jackets, embroidered deco shawls, mid-century dirndl skirts, felt hats, antique silk slips, vintage dancing shoes and handbags. The owner Leslie has twenty years' experience of dealing in antiques and collectable clothing and also has a section on the first floor dedicated to quality antique luggage and sporting goods where you will be greeted by a brightly dressed jockey, a 1950s plinth from the Jockey Club, standing guard over original leather bound suitcases and vintage designer luggage. Leslie has supplied his historical finds to film sets, designers and the cast of Downton Abbey.

Left: A mid-century sofa and a classic Bakelite telephone at **Thirteen Interiors**.

Continue to walk round the ground floor amongst the many booths selling antique jewellery, artworks, vintage crockery, 1950s homeware and kitchenware. By the front staircase you'll see **Sambataro** and their glittering display of twentieth-century decorative lighting, Murano glass and Italian furniture from the likes of Gio Ponti and Carlo Mollino.

Thirteen Interiors, also on the ground floor, trades in late 1940s and mid-century furniture, lighting and smaller vintage items such as classic Bakelite telephones from the 1950s and 60s. From here, take one of the staircases up to the first floor where you'll find a number of lighting specialists in the impressive open plan area, including a gleaming collection of twentieth-century mirrors from **Angela Ball** as well as furniture and interiors. Visit **Christine Murray** for a selection of British, European and South American twenthieth-century lighting, accessories and furniture and an impressive collection of mid-century coloured glass candlesticks.

If Fornasetti ceramics are your cup of tea look no further than **Cupio** for a comprehensive collection of the designer's decorated plates and jars as well as Italian furniture and lighting.

Each dealer is on hand to answer questions and offer information and business cards are available at every point.

Previous pages: A 1950s ribbon evening dress and painted figure of a jockey, both from **Tin Tin Collectables**.
Left: Coloured mirrors and mid-century lighting at **Angela Ball**.

More lighting and mid-century treasures continue; look out for rattan furniture and eclectic vintage from **Travers Antiques** and the delightful collection of paintings from dealer **Robert McKoy** where rows of canvases lean against the wall and stacks of artworks on tables beg to be browsed through. Robert offers a very varied selection of oil paintings and watercolours ranging from the seventeenth to the twentieth century.

Continue up to the second floor for the **Vintage Modes** fashion emporium where stylists and designers in the know scout for fashion and magazine shoots. And for a well-deserved cup of tea take the oak stair case, or the lift, to the third floor Roof Top Kitchen café and terrace for a bird's eye view of Marylebone's rooftops.

Like the department store it once was, Alfies has something for everyone; from vintage Christmas decorations, jewellery, a second-floor fashion emporium and the antiques and specialist collections on the upper and lower floors you'll find it very hard to leave empty-handed.

You may also like

To discover more from the Alfies collective visit **GRAYS ANTIQUES** in the west end for some of the best selections of antique jewellery in London. See page 122.

Portobello Road Antiques Market

NOTTING HILL

Portobello Road, W11
www.portobelloroad.co.uk
Market open Fridays and Saturdays but individual shops and stalls may vary

The painted houses and shop fronts on Portobello Road and surrounding streets of Westbourne Grove and Blenheim Crescent have inspired many authors and filmmakers over the decades. The market and antiques shops draw thousands of visitors each week and although Saturday is the main trading day it's well worth visiting the stalls on the Friday market for vintage clothes and other specialist dealers.

The area of Portobello Road between Chepstow Villas and Elgin Crescent is my favourite strip of the market and where you'll find some of the best indoor arcades and antiques shops such as **Dolphin Arcade** for jewellery and silverware and **Chelsea Galleries** for vintage cookware and copper kitchen moulds.

On Saturdays start at the top end of the market, close to Notting Hill tube, where the boutiques and shops curve round to meet Portobello Road. **Alice's Antiques**, painted an unmissable pillar-box red, is a Dickensian-style curiosity shop filled with vintage treasures where wooden crates, teapots and old enamel signs spill out along the pavement. Venture inside to see their selection of old globes, reclaimed market crates, dolly washtubs, vintage baskets, mirrors and flags. A little further along, at the junction with Westbourne Grove, you'll find the first of the market stalls heaped with a variety of stock ranging from specialist antiques to mid-century finds, books, coins, rare prints, ceramics and all kinds of bric-a-brac.

A stack of 1950s garden chairs and a box old wooden shoes lasts at Portobello Market.

As you walk down Portobello Road look out for individual stalls such as **Fashoda** and their vast collection of vintage prints and rare cigarette picture cards and **Andy Morant,** a specialist collector of lead toys and soldiers; you'll also find collectable and vintage cameras at **Cameras London** and further down the street you'll come across letterpress type at **The Old Printing Shop**. Sweeping down Portobello, the shops and market continue to the indoor antiques arcades and pretty shopping streets of Notting Hill. Take in the atmosphere of the market and be sure to stop at one of the many vibrant cafés, bars and pubs that Portobello has to offer as it stretches all the way down to the Westway overpass.

Portobello Road in Notting Hill is one of the most photographed areas in London with its pastel-painted shop fronts and Regency-era houses.

The Old Cinema

CHISWICK

160 Chiswick High Road, W4 1PR
www.theoldcinema.co.uk

As the name suggests The Old Cinema, on Chiswick high street, is a converted Edwardian picture palace. This stunning building was rescued from demolition in the 1970s and for almost fifty years has provided showroom space for antiques dealers, interior designers and an in-house restoration service.

Among the many dealers at The Old Cinema you will find a fantastic choice of high-end antiques, vintage curiosities, Scandinavian mid-century furniture, textiles from India, carvings from Italy and salvaged shop lights from the USA. Stock is replenished on a regular basis and at any given time you'll come across good quality, large-scale antiques to suit all budgets. There's also a wide selection of smaller vintage items and decorative pieces such as Amish star roof tiles, salvaged garden planters, terracotta urns, dining chairs and tables from different eras, Chesterfield sofas and architectural salvage to name just some of the items for sale. For anyone putting together a look for film sets, restaurants or home renovation projects this place has to be at the top of your list.

Following pages: For specialist, good quality antiques to mid-century furniture and vintage items the Old Cinema is the place to visit. One of the many dealers at The Old Cinema is **Matt Goss**, with his timeless collection of antique furniture and lighting from different eras.

Petersham Nurseries

RICHMOND

Church Lane, Richmond, TW10 7AQ
also at:
31 King Street & Floral Court, Covent Garden, WC2E 9FB
www.petershamnurseries.com

This picturesque plot nestled against a twist in the Thames at Richmond is one of the prettiest spots around. Essentially a nursery with a shop and stylish greenhouse café it has become synonymous with its beautiful meadow setting and kitchen garden surrounded by jasmine and bougainvillea.

At the core of the business is the garden shop where you will find a tastefully edited collection of home and garden items; vintage furniture, mirrors and decorative pieces sourced both in the UK and overseas. From terracotta plant pots to antique dining tables and salvaged cast-iron planters the shop and displays at Petersham never disappoint.

For more of Petersham's whimsical 'secret garden' look you can also visit their central London location in Covent Garden and pick up vintage glassware, antique furniture and one-off handcrafted homewares. **Petersham Covent Garden** has an in-house florist as well as smaller vintage items such as garden pots, vases and decorative pieces for sale in the shop.

CENTRAL LONDON
& THE CITY

Old Spitalfields Market

SPITALFIELDS

16 Horner Square,
Spitalfields, E1 6EW
www.oldspitalfieldsmarket.com
Market open every Thursday

With a trading history dating back to the 1600s there has been a market at Spitalfields since King Charles I granted a licence to sell fresh produce. Today you'll find a rather different set up but it's still a thriving marketplace serving the City of London and every Thursday one of capital's favourite antiques markets pitches its stalls under the shelter of the listed Victorian glass and steel roof.

It is a relaxed atmosphere where a cheery community of traders sell to collectors, stylists, artists and fashion designers and where the colourful East End meets the Georgian history of the City. Here you'll discover some of the best finds in London for small to medium-sized items such as toys, antique jewellery, vintage clothes, Americana, textiles, antique ceramics and cutlery, 1970s kitsch, collectable postcards, books, maps and tinware.

Choose from a beautifully curated collection of hand-picked French vintage and antique mirrors from **Clou Antiques** or the wide selection of vintage clothes at **Jane Reed** (right). Unearth quirky, theatrical finds at **Arabella Clemency** and antique lead soldiers, vintage toys, prints and books at **All Things Counter** (previous page).

Browse between the stalls with a coffee from one of the many food stalls around the outer edge and cast your eye over the choice of French garden furniture, glassware, basketware and apothecary bottles at **Benjamin Antiques** (previous page, right) and 1950s kitchenware and pottery at **Enamelama**. For rare and vintage maps and globes visit **Malby Map**s where you will literally be transported to another world.

You don't have to spend a fortune; as well as antiques you're sure to spot plenty of bargains at one of the bric-a-brac stalls and most traders are open to a friendly haggle.

Henry Pordes Books

CHARING CROSS ROAD

58–60 Charing Cross Road,
WC2H 0BB
www.henrypordesbooks.com

If you've ever read the charming book *84 Charing Cross Road*, by Helene Hanff, based on the correspondence between the author in New York and a member of staff at a bookshop in Charing Cross Road, you'll already be halfway to imagining what the street looked like in its 1930s heyday. Many of the original bookshops that made the street famous have sadly disappeared though several long established second-hand and antiquarian booksellers still remain including Henry Pordes.

At the Leicester Square end of Charing Cross Road, at Henry Pordes, you'll discover a world of vintage and antiquarian books. Literally packed to the ceiling, the shelves groan with every genre from science fiction to art and an enviable selection of beautifully bound Victorian botanical and wildlife books including rare first editions and prized collectables.

Whether you are looking for vintage one-offs or second-hand Penguin paperbacks this rare delight of a bookshop has something to suit all pockets. The staff are very welcoming and on hand to answer any literary enquiries.

Any Amount of Books

CHARING CROSS ROAD

56 Charing Cross Road,
WC2H 0QA
www.anyamountofbooks.com

It's definitely worth taking the time to dip into the extensive collection of vintage paperbacks and collectable hardbacks on the shelves at Any Amount of Books. This second-hand and antiquarian bookshop boasts many rare finds and first edition gems as well as their bargain boxes containing books from £1 upward. It is a charming shop and a real treat to browse its well-stocked shelves.

Grays Antiques

MAYFAIR

58 Davies Street, W1K 5LP
www.graysantiques.com

Grays has been a central London antiques mainstay since 1977 with specialist dealers that include antique textiles, watches and clocks, art deco jewellery, porcelain, paintings, oriental art, luggage and travel accessories, costume jewellery, vintage toys and barware.

Just a stone's throw from Claridges and between the upmarket boutiques of South Molton Street, this handsome terracotta building, originally a Victorian bath showroom, now boasts over 100 individual antiques traders. **Diane & Kati** specialize in antique linen and lace such as dainty Edwardian wedding bags and Victorian embroidery. Amongst the wide choice of antique gems and jewellery you will find **Sylvie Spectrum** with a glittering collection of Victorian silver and gold jewellery including 'Regard' rings – a Victorian trend for spelling the word 'regard' and other secret messages of love by using the initial letters of the gemstones in the item. Spectrum's owner, Nicola, also deals in vintage bracelet charms ranging from horseshoes to snake charmers, frying pans, Buckingham Palace and rainbow-coloured enamel butterfly brooches and pendants ranging from around 1905, shown overleaf.

Browse the dealers in the downstairs section where antiquities such as beautifully detailed Japanese and Chinese porcelain can be seen at **Guest and Gray** as well as etchings and paintings. At **Anders Kaae** expect to be dazzled by diamonds and colourful gemstones with a selection of deco and 1940s jewellery including engagement rings and a jewel-encrusted spider brooch.

Liberty London

OXFORD CIRCUS

Oriental Carpet Department, 4th Floor, Liberty London,
Regent Street (entrance Great Marlborough Street), W1B 5AH
www.libertylondon.com

Liberty's Tudor-revival building is famous for its stunning architecture and interior decoration and was commissioned by its founder, Arthur Lasenby Liberty in the 1920s. It was Liberty's dream to offer his customers beautiful crafts, textiles and unusual finds from around the world. That wish still holds true today with a captivating emporium filled with luxury brands, hand-picked treasures and antiques.

Liberty has stocked antiques since its inception and the Oriental Carpet Department, on the fourth floor, is dedicated to antique carpets, old woven rugs and ceramic and carved objects from the bazaars of Iran and the Hindu Kush mountains. Buyer Bruce Lepere and staff are very friendly and knowledgeable about their subject and happy to show a variety of options and colours.

On the second floor you'll find vintage designer womenswear and wedding dresses and on the ground and lower ground floors a selection of vintage accessories, pre-loved handbags and luggage from designer labels such as Louis Vuitton and Chanel.

And while you are there, take the time to admire the Liberty clock dating from 1924 and the central crystal chandelier, said to be the longest in Europe.

Left & following pages: Liberty's Oriental Carpet department is filled with warmth and exotic colour with antique carpets from around the world.

Word on the Water

KINGS CROSS

York Way, Granary Square, N1C 4LW
www.wordonthewater.co.uk

Jon and Paddy have sold second-hand books from their Dutch barge for the past ten years and have created a glorious Swallows and Amazons old world feel where books beg to be browsed in this unique waterfront setting. Nicknamed the London Book Barge this compact floating bookstore, moored on Regents Canal near Kings Cross, has a wide selection of second-hand stock including contemporary writing, art, classic fiction and photography as well as new books and a popular subscription service for those unable to visit in person.

Step into the barge from the towpath and you will be greeted by the chattering of their rescued African grey parrot (an unwanted Christmas present from a previous owner), and enter through the children's section where a seating area is covered in patterned textiles and cushions. The interior is a charming and eclectic mix of antiques with vintage typewriters, a log burning stove and old leather armchairs neatly positioned by the bookcases. You'll find more books out on deck in shelves fashioned from reclaimed canoes and on the day I visited Jon was unpacking and sorting fresh stock.

Grab a coffee from nearby Coal Drops Yard and enjoy the gentle sway of the water whilst browsing the shelves or visit in the evening for their poetry slams and live acoustic music events staged on the roof.

Finding Inspiration

As a shopkeeper I know how important it is to create an exciting and welcoming environment where visitors are encouraged to interact with the display and be inspired by the ever-changing collection of vintage pieces.

Over the next few pages I take a look at creating vintage displays and take inspiration from favourite stalls and antiques shops, to demonstrate how a few reclaimed objects can uplift the corner of a room or add a small decorative feature, cheaply and without spending a huge amount of time.

It's not difficult to find style ideas at **Petersham Nurseries**, see page 106, where every turn is laden with vintage gardening references and floral details. Starting small, with just a handful of old glass jars, plant pots or even teacups you can style a windowsill or bookshelf with flowers and houseplants like the one, left, at **Petersham Covent Garden**.

To add a touch of rustic charm use objects you may already have at home such as old trowels, paintbrushes, gardening sieves and scraps of fabric or ferret out interesting pieces from flea markets.

Use larger pots like the reclaimed paint bucket and vintage jug shown here, to display fresh and dried flowers and add in old tins, teapots and bottles. Play with different heights to create interest and use pieces of vintage cloth to tie your bunches of flowers like the one pictured.

Another trick is to use antique linens such as hand-embroidered tablecloths, easy to pick up fairly cheaply at vintage fairs, for vintage-style tea parties, and lengths of antique fabric to frame or cover furniture. Or choose a theme such as 'beachcomber' and create a vignette using shells, feathers, driftwood and seaside-inspired imagery.

I could easily lose hours in second-hand bookshops such as Henry Pordes, see page 119, and I always keep an eye out for vintage books at flea markets and antiques fairs. Their faded dust sleeves and worn covers look so attractive when stacked on shelves or tables to create small vignettes. The more battered they are, the better they look, telling their own tales of previous ownership. I especially like cookery, gardening and botanical books as they regularly contain colour plates or have beautifully illustrated front covers. Sometimes they come with little notes in the margins, clippings from newspapers, keepsake recipes and on some occasions, pressed flowers.

Vintage collector and prop stylist Karen Cadman has built an inspiring collection of images using old books, typewriters, newspapers, vintage fabrics and found objects on her Instagram feed, @permillion44.

In the set up shown here Karen has built a story around a vintage book displayed like a small painting. She says her inspiration comes from, 'a timeless combination of vintage finds and seasonal wildflowers, reminiscent of a more simple, slower pace of life'.

You don't need to venture too far to spark ideas – it's sometimes just a matter of looking at what you already have and putting it in a different context.

Start with a favourite postcard from a museum or gallery exhibition, a stack of second-hand records – the sleeves are often a wonderful mix of photography and illustration – or a stash of old photographs and vintage camera and display them on a low table, the corner of a room or somewhere prominent that will catch your eye every now and then.

Many of the stallholders at vintage markets such as **Spitalfields Antiques** (see page 112) have a knack for creating effortlessly stylish displays. Dealer **Arabella Clemency** groups salvaged objects, mementoes and random finds to create individual little stories. It may be a pair of Victorian lace-up slippers, an old painted banjo with Edwardian sheet music and a box of bow ties to create a music hall feel. Or the worn red velvet purse, left, displayed with an ornate Venetian glass mirror, jewelled boxes and a vintage cake decoration. Her love of the unusual, off beat and dramatic is pure inspiration and one that can be referenced at home with a few favourite pieces.

Try grouping paintings, second-hand mirrors and vintage prints, see examples on page 6 and above, or display interesting textures such as reclaimed wooden chopping boards, aged enamel advertising signs, apothecary bottles, second-hand ceramics and shelves layered with colourful china, shown overleaf at **Vintage Heaven** (see page 54).

Directory

NORTH LONDON

Camden Passage Antiques Market
(see page 15)
Camden Passage, Islington, N1 8AE
www.camdenpassageislington.co.uk
The market runs every Wednesday from 10am.
Check individual shop opening times before
heading out.
Includes: **Annie's**, 12, Pierrepont Arcade,
(anniesvintageclothing.co.uk), *(see p. 18)*;
Number One, 1, Pierrepont Arcade, *(see p. 15)*

Flashback Records *(see page 22)*
Islington – 50 Essex Road, N1 8LR
Crouch End – 144 Crouch Hill, N8 9DX
Shoreditch – 131 Bethnal Green Road, E2 7DG
www.flashback.co.uk

Past Caring *(see pages 26)*
54 Essex Road, Islington, N1 8LR

Camden Market *(see page 30)*
Camden Lock Place, Camden Town, NW1 8AF
www.camdenmarket.com
Everyday 10am–late, times may vary for
each business.

Rokit *(see page 32)*
225 Camden High St, Camden Town, NW1 7BU
Also at: Rokit, 101 Brick Lane, E1 6SE
Rokit Originals Boutique, 107 Brick Lane, E1 6SE
Rokit Covent Garden, 42 Shelton Street, WC2H 9HZ
www.rokit.co.uk

The Black Gull Bookshop & Bindery
(see page 34)
70–71 West Yard, Camden Lock Place,
Camden Town, NW1 8AF
www.camdenmarket.com

Patina *(see page 36)*
7 Chatsworth Road, E5 0LH

SOUTH LONDON

Lassco Brunswick House *(see page 42)*
30 Wandsworth Road, Vauxhall, SW8 2LG
www.lassco.co.uk

Flea at Vinegar Yard *(see page 46)*
Vinegar Yard, St Thomas St, Bermondsey,
SE1 3QU
www.flealondon.com
Open weekends, check ahead for venue access.

Vintique London *(see page 48)*
Unit 13 Station Passage, Queen's Road,
SE15 2JR
www.vintiquelondon.co.uk
Open Saturday 10am–5pm, Sunday 11am–5pm

EAST LONDON

Paper Dress Vintage *(see page 52)*
352a Mare St, E8 1HR,
www.paperdressvintage.co.uk

Vintage Heaven *(see page 54)*
82 Columbia Rd, E2 7QB
www.vintageheaven.co.uk

B Southgate Vintage *(see page 58)*
4 The Courtyard, Ezra St, E2 7RH
www.bsouthgate.co.uk

Town House *(see page 62)*
5 Fournier Street, E1 6QE
www.townhousespitalfields.com

Retrouvé *(see page 70)*
23 Broadway Market, E8 4PH
61 Wilton Way, E8 1BS
www.retrouvevintage.co.uk

Pure White Lines at Mare St. Market
(*see page 74*)
117 Mare Street, E8 4RU
www.purewhitelines.com
www.marestreetmarket.com

Hunky Dory (*see page 78*)
226 Brick Lane, E1 6SA
www.hunkydoryvintage.com

Straw London (*see page 80*)
126 Columbia Road, E2 7RG
www.strawlondon.co.uk

WEST LONDON

Alfies Antique Market (*see page 86*)
13–25 Church St, NW8 8DT
alfiesantiques.com
Includes: **Tin Tin Collectables** (*see p. 87*); **Thirteen Interiors** (*see pp. 86 and 91*); **Sambataro** (*see p. 91*); **Angela Ball** (*see p. 91*); **Christine Murray** (*see p. 91*); **Cupio** (*see p. 91*); **Travers Antiques** (*see p.92*); **Robert McKoy** (*see p. 92*); **Vintage Modes** (*see p. 92*)

Portobello Road Antiques Market
(*see page 94*)
Portobello Road, W11
Market open Fridays and Saturdays but individual shops and stalls may vary.
www.portobelloroad.co.uk
Includes: **Dolphin Arcade** (*see p. 95*); **Chelsea Galleries** (*see p. 95*); **Alice's Antiques** (*see p. 96*); **Fashoda** (*see p. 100*); **Andy Morant** (*see p. 100*); **Cameras London** (*see p. 100*); **The Old Printing Shop** (*see p.100*)

The Old Cinema (*see page 102*)
160 Chiswick High Road, W4 1PR
www.theoldcinema.co.uk
Includes: **Matt Goss** (*see p. 103*)

Petersham Nurseries (*see page 106*)
Church Lane, Richmond, TW10 7AQ
Also at: 31 King Street & Floral Court,
Covent Garden, WC2E 9FB
www.petershamnurseries.com

CENTRAL LONDON & THE CITY

Old Spitalfields Market (*see page 112*)
16 Horner Square, Spitalfields, E1 6EW
www.oldspitalfieldsmarket.com
Includes: **Clou Antiques** (*see p. 116*); **Arabella Clemency** (*see p. 116*); **Jane Reed** (*see p. 116*); **All Things Counter**, www.allthingscounter.com, (*see p. 116*); **Benjamin Antiques** (*see p. 116*); **Enamelama** (*see p. 116*); **Malby Maps**, www.malbymaps.com, (*see p. 116*)

Henry Pordes Books (*see page 118*)
58–60 Charing Cross Road, WC2H 0BB
www.henrypordesbooks.com

Any Amount of Books (*see page 120*)
56 Charing Cross Road, WC2H 0QA
www.anyamountofbooks.com

Grays Antiques (*see page 122*)
58 Davies Street, W1K 5LP
www.graysantiques.com
Includes: **Anders Kaae** (www.anderskaae.com) (*see p. 124*); **Guest and Gray** (*see p.124*); **Diane & Kati** (*see p. 123*); **Sylvie Spectrum** (*see p.123*)

Liberty London (*see page 126*)
Oriental Carpet Department, 4th Floor,
Liberty London, Regent Street (entrance Great Marlborough Street), W1B 5AH
www.libertylondon.com

Word on the Water (*see page 130***)**
York Way, Granary Square, N1C 4LW
www.wordonthewater.co.uk

Acknowledgements

I would like to thank all at Pimpernel Press for making this book happen especially to Jo and Gail for the magic and to my editor Anna . . . it's been a real pleasure working with you again. Very special thanks to Becky for the design and to Emma for press.

Huge thanks goes to each and every shop and market mentioned in the book for your time and generosity and for giving me access to your wonderful stories and collections. Especially to Nick at Lassco, Fiona at Townhouse, Mark at Flashback Records, all at Rokit, Bruce and Matt at Liberty, the staff at Petersham Nurseries and Annie at Annie's Vintage. A massive thank you, for insights and contributions from Paula Flynn at The Shopkeepers, Rosie Shennan, Cilla Shrieves, Ginny Burnett, Karen Cadman, Dvora, Siobhan Ferguson, Will at The Old Cinema, Matt Goss and Emily at Straw London. Also to Leslie at Tin Tin Collectables, the staff at Henry Pordes Books, Patina, Ben Southgate, Margaret at Vintage Heaven, Elizabeth, Arabella and Claire at Spitalfields Antiques Market, Leigh Chappell Flowers and all at Mare Street Market. I've met so many inspiring people whilst working on the book and it's been a joy to finally meet some of you in person. Thank you!

Photo Credits